See for Yourself

Hearing

See for Yourself

Hearing

Brenda Walpole
Photographs by Barrie Watts

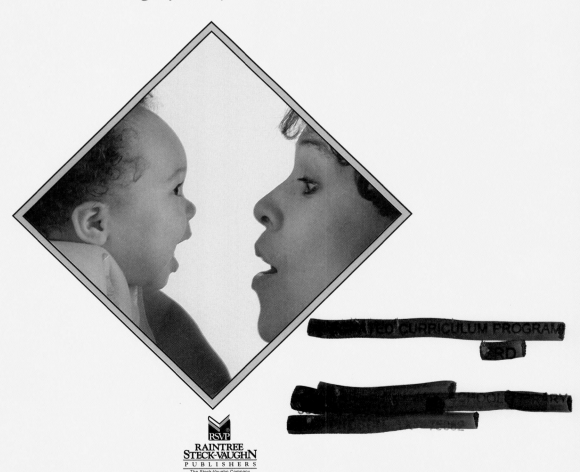

RSVP
RAINTREE
STECK-VAUGHN
PUBLISHERS
The Steck-Vaughn Company

Austin, Texas

Published by Raintree Steck-Vaughn Publishers, an imprint of Steck-Vaughn Company

Editor: Kathy DeVico
Project Manager: Amy Atkinson
Electronic Production: Scott Melcer

All photographs by Barrie Watts except for:
p. 10 John Birdsall; p. 11 Zefa Picture Library (UK) Ltd; p. 14 Michael Leach/NHPA; p. 20 David Woodfall/NHPA; p. 21 Georgette Douma/Planet Earth; p. 24 (main photo) John Birdsall; p. 24 (inset) Ann Roman Picture Library; p. 25 Custom Medical Stock Photo; p. 26 Eye Ubiquitous; p. 27 Saturn Stills/Science Photo Library.

Library of Congress Cataloging-in-Publication Data
Walpole, Brenda.
    Hearing / Brenda Walpole; photographs by Barrie Watts.
        p.   cm. — (See for yourself)
    Includes index.
    Summary: Introduces the concept of hearing and suggests activities which reinforce the understanding of this sense.
    ISBN 0-8172-4217-1
    1. Hearing — Juvenile literature.   [1. Hearing.   2. Senses and sensation.]   I. Watts, Barrie, ill.   II. Title.   III. Series.
    QP462.2.W35   1997
    612.8'5 — dc20   96-11077
                                                                        CIP
                                                                        AC

Printed and bound in the United States
1 2 3 4 5 6 7 8 9 0 LB 99 98 97 96

Contents

Sounds All Around Us 6

Our Ears 8

Learning to Speak 10

Making Sounds 12

Sounds Animals Make 14

Vibrations 16

Guitar Strings 18

What We Cannot Hear 20

Recording Sounds 22

Hearing Aids 24

Protecting Our Ears 26

More Things to Do 28

Index 29

Notes for Parents and Teachers 30

Sounds All Around Us

How can you tell where you are, if your eyes are closed?

If you listen carefully, your ears will tell you. The sounds of cars and trucks can mean that you are close to a main road. But if you are by the ocean, you hear the waves and seagulls calling.

Sounds are loudest when they are close to you. As a train approaches, you might hear it rumbling softly in the distance. But when the train is very close, you will hear a loud roaring sound.

Which room in your house is the noisiest? Write down all the things that you can hear there. Where is the quietest place you know?

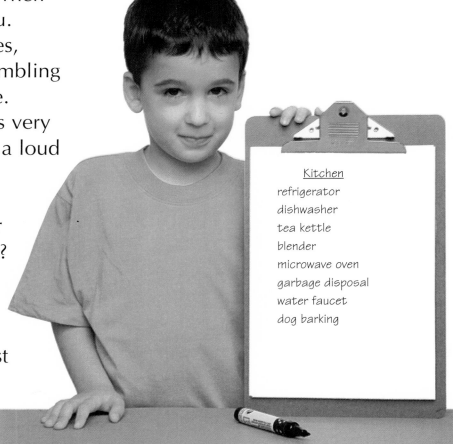

Kitchen
refrigerator
dishwasher
tea kettle
blender
microwave oven
garbage disposal
water faucet
dog barking

Our Ears

You can hear sounds when they enter your ears.
Your brain then figures out what the sounds are.

Your ears can also tell you where a sound is coming from.
The ear that is closer to a sound will hear it before
the other ear.

Turn on a radio. Now close your eyes, and keep them
closed. Ask a friend to gently spin you around a few times.
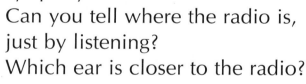
Can you tell where the radio is,
just by listening?
Which ear is closer to the radio?

Learning to Speak

We learn to speak by listening to the people around us.

At first, babies can only make simple sounds.
Then they start to copy the speech sounds
that grown-ups make. They learn to speak
by copying and then practicing words. By
the age of two, children begin to put words
together to make sentences.

It is important for parents to talk to their babies.
Can you guess why?

Some people are
born deaf. It is very
difficult for them to
learn to speak.
How are the
children in the
small picture able
to understand
each other?

Making Sounds

We can make all sorts of sounds for others to hear.
We can talk, sing, whistle, or shout.
What other sounds can we make?

To speak, you must move your lips and tongue.
If you make a circle with your lips, you can say "oo,"
but you have to change the shape of your mouth to say "la."
Look in a mirror and say "cheese."
What shapes do your lips make now?

When you speak, the voice
box in your throat vibrates.
Put your fingers lightly on your
throat, and you can feel it.
Make high and squeaky
sounds, like a mouse, then low
and rumbly sounds.
What happens to your voice
box as you make each
different sound?

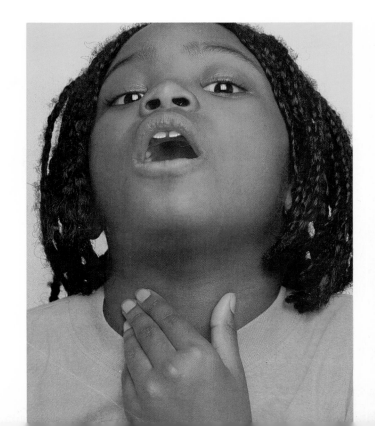

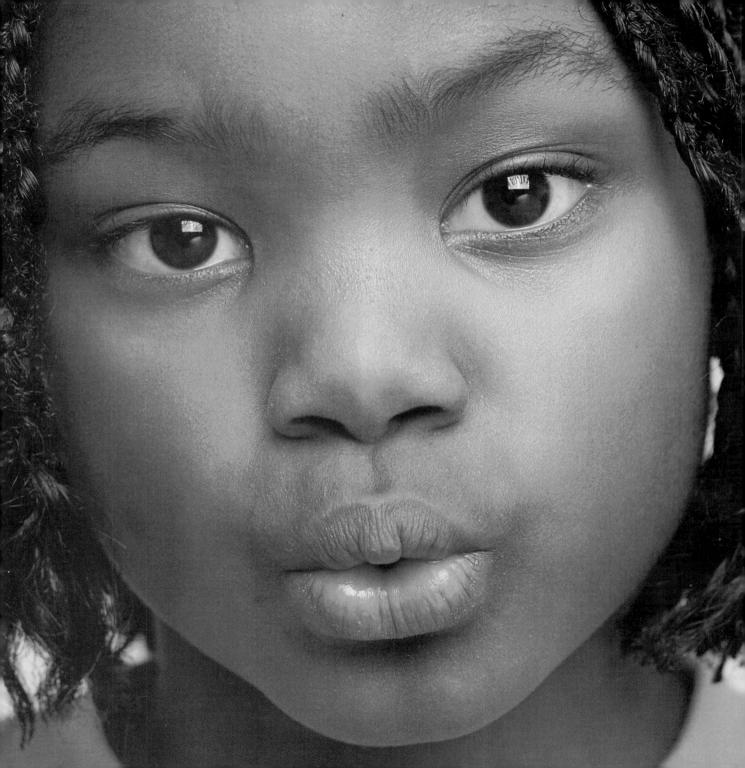

Sounds Animals Make

You talk to your friends to tell them what you are doing and how you feel. Animals do the same thing.

Some birds sing early in the morning. Their songs tell other birds where they are or to stay away.
Each kind of bird has a different song. Have you heard the songs of a pigeon, a cuckoo, or a blackbird?

Our pets make sounds that we learn to understand.
A cat meows to tell its owner it is hungry and purrs when it is happy.
A dog will often bark when a stranger comes to its home.

Vibrations

If you hit a cymbal or pluck a guitar string, you can see each vibrate. At the same time, they make a sound. The sound dies away as the vibrations stop. All musical instruments have parts that vibrate as they are played.

When a drummer hits a drum, the drum skin vibrates up and down. You can make your own drum by stretching a piece of plastic wrap tightly over a plastic bowl. Put some tape on the edges of the plastic wrap to keep it in place. Tap it gently, and listen to the sound. Sprinkle a few grains of rice on the top, and tap it again. Why do the grains jump up and down?

Tap harder, and see what happens to the grains. How can you make the sound louder or softer? What happens to the grains as you do?

16

Guitar Strings

When you pluck a guitar string, it vibrates and makes a sound. The sound goes inside the guitar through the hole in the middle. The sound echoes inside, which makes it last longer.

You can make your own guitar. Gather a few rubber bands for the strings. Try to find some thick ones and some thin ones, like the strings on a real guitar. Stretch the bands across an empty shoebox or cookie tin.

Pluck the rubber bands, one at a time. Which ones make lower notes, and which ones make higher notes?

We say that deep, rumbly sounds are low-pitched. They come from the thickest strings, which vibrate slowly. High, squeaky sounds are high-pitched. They come from thinner strings, which vibrate quickly.

What We Cannot Hear

Many animals can hear a wider range of sounds than we can.

Whales speak to each other in slow songs with notes that are too low in pitch for us to hear. The sounds travel for hundreds of miles through the water. A humpback whale, like the one in the big picture, sings a song that lasts for about half an hour. Then it starts the song all over again.

We also cannot hear the very high-pitched sounds that dog whistles make. But shepherds use dog whistles to call to their sheepdogs as they round up sheep.

Recording Sounds

Cassette tapes, records, and compact discs have sounds recorded onto them. The sounds are in a sort of code. The code on a tape can be turned back into music by a tape player, and the sounds come out of the speakers. If you rest your hand gently on a speaker, you can feel the vibrations.

Sing or talk into a microphone, and record your own voice using a tape recorder. Now play back the tape. Does your recorded voice sound different from your normal voice? Which voice do you think is more like the one your friends hear when you speak to them?

Hearing Aids

Some people are born deaf. Others lose their hearing as they get older. Many people use hearing aids to help them hear. Modern hearing aids contain a tiny microphone that makes sounds louder. Can you see the hearing aid in the big picture?

One hundred years ago, hearing aids looked like the one in the small picture. They were called ear trumpets. The person who used the ear trumpet would put the narrow end in his or her ear and turn the open end toward whatever he or she wanted to hear.

Try making an ear trumpet. Roll a piece of thin cardboard into a cone. Put it to your ear, and listen. The cone will collect sounds and direct them into your ear.

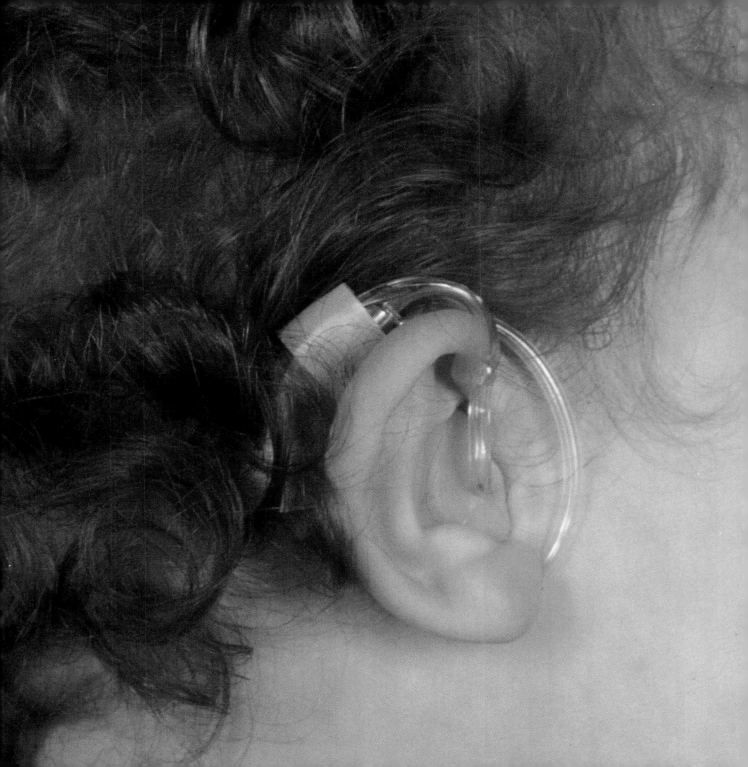

Protecting Our Ears

A sudden, very loud sound, such as an explosion, can hurt the ear and make a person deaf. Loud sounds that go on for a long time are also bad for our ears. Once our ears are badly damaged, they may never hear properly again.

Sometimes people cannot hear well when they have a cold or an infection, or if their ears are blocked with wax. A doctor will look for such a problem by shining a tiny flashlight into their ears. He or she can then help to make the problem better.

People who live near highways or airports often have double-glazed windows to cut down on the noise.

How do you protect your ears when you are in a noisy place? What should people do to protect their ears if they have noisy jobs?

More Things to Do

1. Animal ears
We can't move our ears, but many animals can turn their ears to hear sounds from other directions. Rabbits have upright ears that can turn to listen for danger. Cup your hands around the backs of your ears. Can you hear better like this? Move your hands around, and see what sounds you can pick up.

2. Different drums
Tap the plastic wrap "skin" on the drum from page 16. Can you figure out why the sound stops if you lay your finger on the plastic wrap? Try making drums with bigger or smaller bowls, or bowls made from wood or metal. Do they all sound the same?

3. Making yourself understood
You saw how to make an ear trumpet on page 24. Try speaking through the ear trumpet to a friend across the room. Can you explain why the trumpet makes sounds clearer? People who cannot hear and cannot use hearing aids can learn to lip-read and use sign language. Try having a chat with a friend without making a sound.

Index

This index will help you find some
of the important words in this book.

animals	14, 15, 20
deaf	10, 24, 26
ear	6, 8, 24, 26
ear trumpet	24
hearing aid	24
high-pitched	18, 20
lips	12
low-pitched	18, 20
microphone	22, 24
musical instruments	16
radio	8
recording	22
songs	14, 20
talk	10, 12, 14, 20
tongue	12
vibrate	12, 16, 18
vibrations	16, 22
voice box	12

Notes for Parents and Teachers

These notes will give you some additional information about the senses and suggest some more activities you might like to try with the children.

Pages 6–9
You could make a sound story for the children. Tape a series of sounds; for example, a door closing, a car starting up, music from the car radio, etc. Now ask the children to try to reconstruct the events from the tape.

Pages 8–9
Sounds are vibrations of molecules in the air. These vibrations enter the ear, and are channeled down the ear canal to the eardrum, a thin membrane of skin. The eardrum vibrates in turn, and passes on the vibrations to three small bones—the hammer, anvil, and stirrup. They are located in an air-filled cavity of the middle ear. These bones pass the vibrations on to a second membrane, the oval window, which is part of a fluid-filled cavity, the cochlea. Tiny hairs inside the cochlea convert the vibrations into electrical signals. These signals are then sent to the brain, which interprets them and figures out what the sounds are.

Pages 10–11
Children who are completely deaf from birth are unable to hear themselves speak or hear the speech of others. They have to learn by watching and copying lip movements of people who are speaking. Then they have to practice controlling their own breathing and vocal cords to form words.

Pages 12–13
Sound travels five times faster through water than air. Molecules of water are closer together than air molecules, so they transmit vibrations more efficiently. Solids, such as wood, transmit sound very well because their molecules are even closer together. The children could try lightly scratching on a tabletop with their fingernails. The sound will be virtually inaudible through the air, but they will be able to hear it easily by pressing an ear to the table.

Pages 16–19
Children can investigate how the vibration of air causes sound. They should set up a row of identical glass bottles and fill up each with a different amount of water. By blowing across the mouth of each bottle, or tapping its side, they can make different notes. Low notes will come from a bottle that contains only a little water, thus allowing a large volume of air to vibrate inside the bottle. In bottles that contain more water, there are smaller areas left in which the air can vibrate, and high notes will be produced.

30